The Hats We Wear

Kela J. Miller

ISBN 979-8-89043-368-8 (paperback)
ISBN 979-8-89043-369-5 (digital)

Christian Faith Publishing
832 Park Avenue
Meadville, PA 16335
www.christianfaithpublishing.com

Printed in the United States of America

To my loving husband and my two beautiful children
for their never-ending support and love.

Who am I?

I am someone who wears a lot of hats…

A whole car full, in fact.

The streets are busy as the sun comes up in the east. I look around, and I see people rushing…to their jobs and through their lives. I spend my days helping these people. I help them by driving them to their destinations. Helping people makes me happy. Helping people makes me feel good. I feel, in a small way, like I am important, and I have helped make their day better.

One day, I helped a man get his wife to a hospital so they could deliver their new baby girl. Another day, I helped a construction worker get to his job site when his truck had broken down. Today, I helped a lady get her groceries home from the market. Each day is new and different, but each day is rewarding in its own special way.

As I turn off my taxi light for the night, I pull into my driveway and take my cabbie hat off. I lay it on the front seat of the car as I grab my family hat. The porch light is on and seems to be calling my name. I wear my family hat with tired eyes all the way to the front door of my house where I am greeted by my three beautiful children. Hugs and kisses all around. That never fails to remind me to wear my family hat with a little more pride.

My wife is cooking supper in the kitchen. It smells amazing. We sit around the table, and we talk about our day. The kids tell me about their school friends and about games they played outside. I am thankful that our family is all together as the day ends.

I have a sleeping hat around here somewhere. I better find it and put it on. Morning comes early, and a cabbie's job is never done.

Who am I?
I am someone who wears a lot of hats…
A whole shop full, in fact.

The smell in the room is hard to ignore because the ovens are on and the sugar is poured. It feels like a fairytale to watch all the ingredients come together. All the pretty colors and flowers that are used to decorate cakes. This shop also has breads and cookies and even bones for your dog. The cookies are big, and the cakes seem so tall. As you peer in the oven, you see the bread rise to the rim of their pans as if they want to jump out and play. As the cakes get stacked, taller and taller, you feel like they are the king of the shop.

I own a bakery, and today is my niece's birthday party. I look at the clock. Half past three… I can't be late; I am bringing the cake. The hat I wear all day is a baker's hat. It is white and tall and very clean. I have a girl who works for me, and when she is in the shop, I have to switch to a boss's hat. When she is busy or gone for the day, I get to serve the customers with my cashier hat, but it is not as pretty.

The birthday cake is done and ready to go. I take off my baker's hat and grab the cake and my keys. The party is at five o'clock, and the hat I will wear is pointy, colorful, and fun.

Who am I?

I am someone who wears a lot of hats…

A whole classroom full, in fact.

A-1

The classroom fills up as the morning bell rings. Students' voices bounce around in the air. I hear stories of the evening before and the scores of their favorite video games. I hear conversations of frustration and others of joy. This is my classroom. I teach math.

Actually, I teach students. I teach them about self-control, forgiveness, love, and the true meaning of friendship. In my classroom, students feel safe. They know I will listen, but they also know I will scold. They can bring me their troubles or leave them at the door. Somewhere in there, we also manage to learn a few strategies in math.

RING!!
Welcome to Math! Class
1/4 =

Welcome to M
Class
I'm Listening

It isn't my job to be their mother, to be their friend, or to be their babysitter. More times than not, I find myself setting my teacher hat on my desk and picking up another to help my students get through their day. My desk is full of hats, hats I wear as needed. My desk also has pencils, erasers, notebooks, and scissors. It has Band-Aids and tissues and snacks for those in need. My students know they can count on me, and I do my best not to let them down. I am not perfect, but I am a person that cares, and I wear a lot of hats. Who am I? I am a teacher!

Who am I?

I am someone who wears a lot of hats…

A whole house full, in fact.

One hat for me and one hat for you. I have a lot of hats; that's true. Why do I wear so many hats? I use them to take care of you.

When your bike falls over as you try a new stunt, and you skin your knee, I grab my nurse's hat as I rush to bandage your wounds. When you come to me in desperation because doing homework is not where you want to be, I grab my teacher hat to help you multiply 80 times 3. When your stomach is growling and says that it is time to eat, I whip up some dinner with my chef hat tucked in my apron belt.

And before you go to bed, I give you lots of kisses and a great big bear hug. The hat I wear for that is full of tender loving care. All day long, my hats change as needed, but my favorite hats are the ones that let me be with you. This is our home, and I am your mom!

I
LOVE
YOU

How many hats do I have? A whole heart full!

About the Author

Kela J. Miller is a native Texan with an undergraduate degree in behavioral science. She grew up traveling with her family where she was able to meet new people and see new places. She soon found that studying people's behaviors interested her. As she studied different behaviors, she also became interested in the individual's lives. Each place seemed to bring new types of people and new things to observe. She noticed that each character seemed to take on a life of its own. In this book, Miller celebrates the roles we play as individuals with fun hats but allows each character the flexibility to choose their hats, as needed.

www.ingramcontent.com/pod-product-compliance
Lightning Source LLC
Chambersburg PA
CBHW040156110726
48005CB00018B/2781